A PERFECT FIT

How Lena "Lane" Bryant Changed the Shape of Fashion

Mara Rockliff

Illustrated by Juana Martinez-Neal

CLARION BOOKS | *An Imprint of HarperCollinsPublishers* | Boston New York

ena's family was not as large as others in the village,
but for her it was a perfect fit.
Her grandfather taught her to read and write.

Her grandmother taught her to drape and snip and stitch. Lena loved her grandparents. Still, life was hard. She dreamed of following her older sister to America.

In America, there was no czar to say that Jewish children couldn't go to school. In America, a girl like Lena could work hard and earn success.

Success! How would it look—as elegant as lace? How would it feel—as comfortable as silk? Certainly, it wouldn't squeeze and pinch like being poor.

Her grandfather smiled. If she could help another person, he told Lena, that would be *real* success.

When Lena was sixteen, some distant relatives offered to take her with them to America. Lena sewed herself a special outfit for the journey.

After many long days on the rough ocean, they arrived at last . . . and Lena found out that the relatives expected her to marry their son!

Lena told them she would pay back every penny for her ticket. But she would only marry when she found a perfect fit.

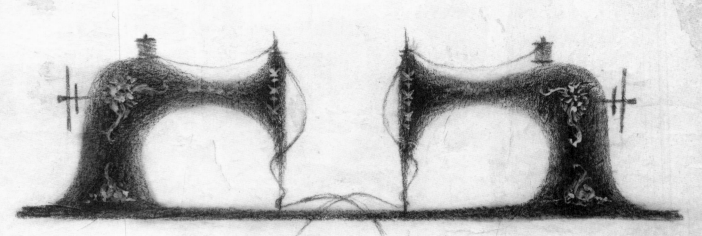

In New York, Lena's sister helped her find a job, sewing from dawn till dusk for one dollar a week.

Lena could not believe her luck.

Lace! Ribbons! Silk!

Most wonderful of all—sewing *machines*!

Lena worked hard and learned fast. Soon, she earned five dollars a week, then ten, then more. She saved enough to pay the relatives back for her ticket to America.

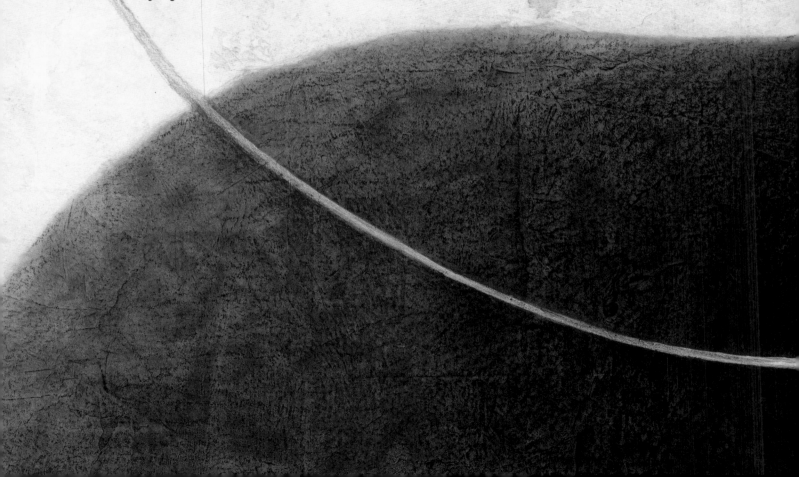

She even found
time for English
lessons.
And she studied
fashion, in the
magazines and
on the streets.

At a lecture, Lena met an older man named David Bryant. He was elegant, yet comfortable—a perfect fit.

Lena and David were happy together. They had a baby. But soon after, David suddenly got sick and died.

Other than a pair of diamond earrings, David's wedding gift, Lena had nothing left.

She pawned her earrings, used the money to buy a sewing machine, and set to work.

Lena never used a pattern or a tape measure. She simply draped and snipped and stitched. Yet, somehow, Lena's gowns fit better than those made by anybody else.

One day, a customer came in with an unusual
request. She was going to have a baby. Could Lena
make a gown that would grow bigger with her belly,
so that it would never squeeze or pinch?

Lena had never heard of such a thing. Who had?

But she remembered her grandfather's words.
Here was a chance to help another person
through her work.

So, she draped and snipped and stitched, and made a gown of silk and lace—with room to grow. It was elegant. It was comfortable. And it was a success.

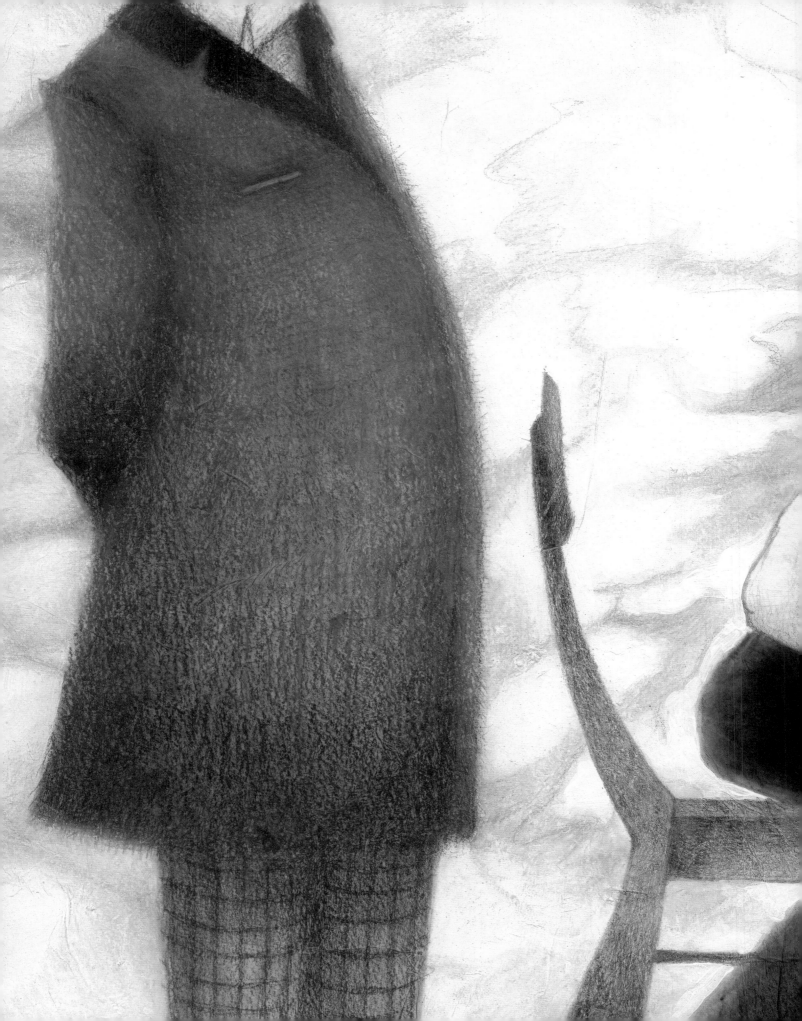

Soon, Lena had to rent a bigger shop and hire more people to help her sew.

She even went to open up a bank account. The big, fancy bank made her so nervous, she mixed up the English letters of her name. Instead of *Lena*, she signed *Lane*.

Lane Bryant

Now there were bigger, faster sewing machines that could make dozens of dresses at a time. Instead of having a dress made to order, women could simply walk into a store and pick one out.

There was just one problem.

All the dress patterns were the same shape.
But all women were not.

Lena got to work.
She draped . . .
She snipped . . .

And the big, fast machines stitched elegant,
comfortable clothes that didn't squeeze or pinch.

Everyone said Lena was a great success.
And when she thought about her grandfather,
she knew that it was true.

AUTHOR'S NOTE

Lena Himmelstein was born in 1879 in Rietavas, Lithuania. Her mother died ten days later, and Lena and her older sister, Annie, were raised by their grandparents. Russian persecution and a lack of opportunities for Jews led first Annie, then Lena, to escape to the United States.

As a teenage immigrant, Lena worked with her sister in a sweatshop on the Lower East Side of Manhattan. Despite the long hours and low pay, she was "ecstatic over the loveliness" of lace and ribbon trimmings, as she later recalled, and quickly learned to use "that fabulous wonder, the sewing machine."

In 1899, she married David Bryant, a jeweler who died soon after the birth of their son, Raphael. Working with the baby on her lap, she sewed dresses for wealthy customers, which she delivered personally to their homes, often waiting hours to be paid so she could buy more fabric. "I had a hunger for beautiful things," she once told an interviewer. "I wanted to do fine sewing on fine materials. I would search through the stores for bits of remnants of fine satins and crepes and bits of lace which I could pick up for a few cents."

1920s

Lena's business grew through word of mouth, especially after she created an expandable maternity dress for a customer who did not want to sit at home alone simply because she had nothing presentable to wear.

Lena's second husband, Albert Malsin, joined her in running the business, and she continued to work after the births of their three children, Theodore, Helen, and Arthur.

1950s

Responding to complaints from customers who couldn't find comfortable, stylish clothes, Albert collected thousands of women's measurements, from which Lena designed clothing for different body types. Lane Bryant became famous for introducing what would later be known as "plus-size" fashions, eventually also adding clothing for tall and petite women.

1980s

2000s

Lena's company was one of the first to offer employee benefits, including health coverage, pensions, and profit sharing, along with scholarships and life insurance. Customers who lost their wardrobes in disasters such as tornadoes and fires were sent free replacements, and after World War II, Lane Bryant stores shipped clothing by the ton to European refugees.

By the time of Lena's death in 1951, the company employed thousands of workers in its mail-order business and stores across the country. Lane Bryant stayed in the family until 1982, when it was sold to a company called The Limited. As of 2021, it had changed hands several times and was owned by Premium Apparel LLC.

All her life, Lena recalled her grandfather, a rabbi, saying, "Any work that helps another human being has dignity. The only real success comes from filling a human need." She saw helping people as the best part of her work—along with silk and lace.

2020s

SELECTED SOURCES

Atlanta Constitution. "Immigrant Girl with an Idea." November 17, 1946.

Bryant, Lane. "They Call Me 'Success Story'" in *Guideposts: Personal Messages of Inspiration and Faith,* ed. Norman Vincent Peale (New York: Prentice-Hall, Inc., 1948).

Decatur Herald Sun. "Lena Himmelstein Sold Wedding Gift on Success Road." August 13, 1950.

Hendrix, Hedda. "The American Dream" in *Pisces with Yeast Rising* (Bloomington, IN: Xlibris, 2002).

Mahoney, Tom. "Lane Bryant: Maternity and Special Size Fashion Pioneer" in *The Great Merchants* (New York: Harper & Brothers, 1955).

New York Times. "Lane Bryant Dies; Founder of Chain." September 27, 1951.

Printers' Ink: A Journal for Advertisers. "A Mail-order Business That Proved the Stepping-stone to a Women's Specialty Chain." August 10, 1916.

St. Louis Post-Dispatch. "Success Story of a Seamstress." February 8, 1948.

St. Louis Post-Dispatch Daily Magazine. "The Success of a Seamstress." August 19, 1938.

To Kate, an editor who is a perfect fit —M.R.

To mi Lita, who had a shop where she draped, snipped, and stitched while
raising her three. And to her reunion with her perfect fit late in life. —J.M.N.

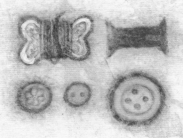

Clarion Books is an imprint of HarperCollins Publishers.

A Perfect Fit

Library of Congress Cataloging-in-Publication Data has been applied for.
ISBN: 978-0-358-12543-3

The illustrations in this book were done in acrylics, colored pencils,
pastels, linocuts, and fabric on hand-textured paper.
The text type was set in Aged Book.
The display type was set in Elise.
Designed by Whitney Leader-Picone

Manufactured in Italy
RTLO 10 9 8 7 6 5 4 3 2 1
4500842810

First Edition

DISASTERS

Ned Halley

SCHOLASTIC INC.
New York Toronto London Auckland Sydney
Mexico City New Delhi Hong Kong Buenos Aires

Editor: Jonathan Stroud
Designer: Veneta Altham
Picture manager: Jane Lambert
Cover illustration: David O'Connor
Indexer: Sue Lightfoot

ISBN 0-439-33873-5

12 11 10 9 8 7 6 5 4 3 2 1   1 2 3 4 5 6/0

Printed in the U.S.A.   14

First Scholastic printing, October 2001

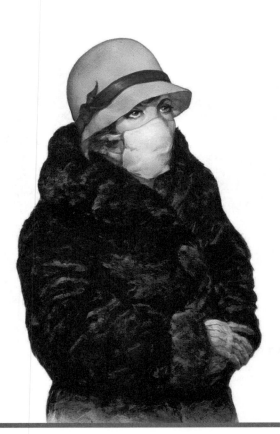

CONTENTS

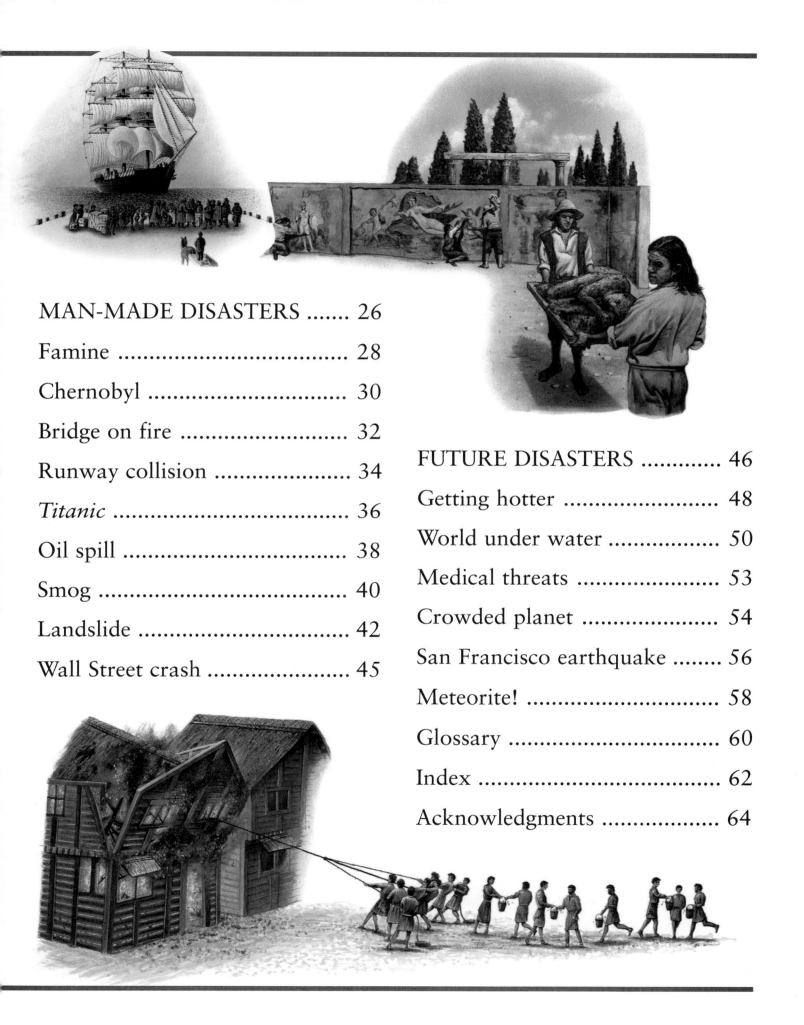

NATURAL DISASTERS

It's a dangerous world. We try to make it safe for ourselves, but wild weather and violent geological events are simply beyond our control. When tornadoes or earthquakes strike populated places, they can spell disaster.

Are natural calamities more common now than they were in the past? News coverage can make it seem so, but it is not nature that's changing—it is us. Since 1900, the world's population has tripled and the built-up areas of the Earth have increased five times in size. Regions prone to disastrous events are now densely populated. Today, more than half of all people live in areas that are at constant risk of flooding.

Whether through optimism or necessity, people often ignore very real dangers. We crowd into cities such as San Francisco and Tokyo, which we know

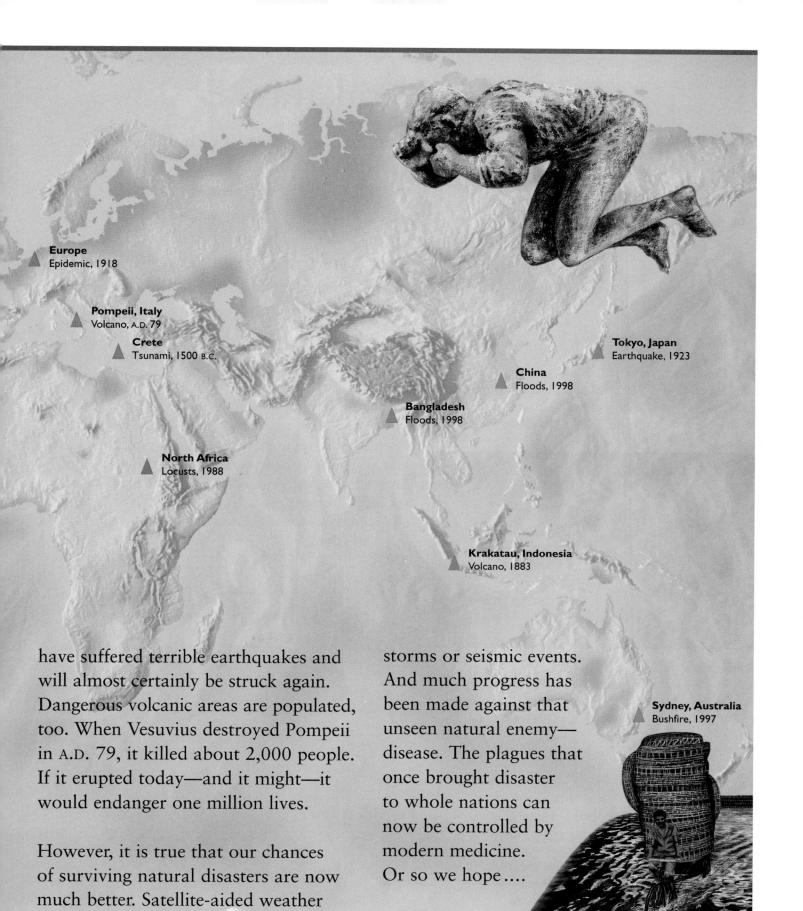

Europe
Epidemic, 1918

Pompeii, Italy
Volcano, A.D. 79

Crete
Tsunami, 1500 B.C.

Tokyo, Japan
Earthquake, 1923

China
Floods, 1998

Bangladesh
Floods, 1998

North Africa
Locusts, 1988

Krakatau, Indonesia
Volcano, 1883

Sydney, Australia
Bushfire, 1997

have suffered terrible earthquakes and will almost certainly be struck again. Dangerous volcanic areas are populated, too. When Vesuvius destroyed Pompeii in A.D. 79, it killed about 2,000 people. If it erupted today—and it might—it would endanger one million lives.

However, it is true that our chances of surviving natural disasters are now much better. Satellite-aided weather forecasting and underground sensor systems can give warnings of imminent storms or seismic events. And much progress has been made against that unseen natural enemy— disease. The plagues that once brought disaster to whole nations can now be controlled by modern medicine. Or so we hope....

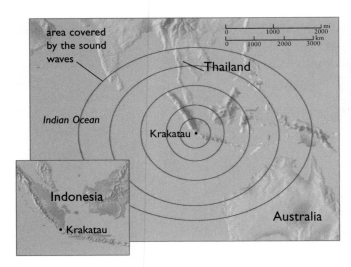

Krakatau

The volcanic eruption of Indonesia's Krakatau Island on August 27, 1883, was the most violent explosion in history—up to 10,000 times the power of the first atomic bomb. The shock waves shook the entire planet and circled the globe seven times. The explosion sounded like the roar of heavy artillery to people nearly 2,000 miles away and ash fell worldwide.

The biggest bang in history
The huge explosion was heard over one twelfth of the surface of the Earth. Traveling at the speed of sound, it took two or more hours to reach Australia and Thailand—and four hours before it was heard on the island of Rodrigues, 3,000 miles to the west.

Tides of destruction
Krakatau was uninhabited, but 36,380 people on the surrounding islands were killed. Many were buried under millions of tons of burning rocks and ash hurled out by the blast. But most died in the 160 villages that were deluged by the giant waves set off by the explosion. Tides caused by the waves snapped the anchor chains of ships moored at ports in Chile, on the other side of the world.

Darkness at noon
Ash from big eruptions forms dense clouds and can block out the sun. This photograph was taken after the eruption of Mt. Pinatubo in the Philippines in 1991—at noon.

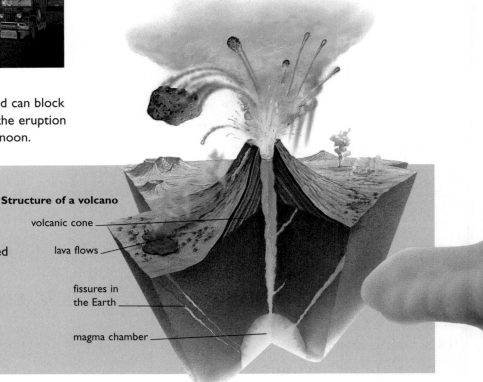

Pressure cooker
The first explosions in Krakatau's three-day eruption opened up the volcano's magma chamber to the sea. Water rushed in through fissures and reacted with molten rock to cause a huge buildup of steam pressure. The resulting blast blew the mountain cone to pieces, spewing out red-hot rocks the size of houses.

Structure of a volcano

volcanic cone

lava flows

fissures in the Earth

magma chamber

Big blast
The Statue of Liberty, which stands 260 feet high, is shown to scale.

Fiery avalanche
The eruption blew Vesuvius's whole cone to smithereens, creating pyroclastic flows—avalanches of scorching ash and dust. At terrifying speeds of up to 100 mph, the flows rolled down the volcano's shattered slopes, straight into the town of Pompeii. People in the streets and houses choked and burned to death as they fled. Victims were quickly entombed by the ash, which continued to rain down for two days, burying everything to the depth of a two-story building.

Vesuvius

In A.D. 79, the Roman citizens of Pompeii were enjoying the good life. The seaside town, said to have been founded 500 years earlier by the mythical hero Hercules, was famed for its beautiful art and buildings. Vineyards on the fertile slopes of nearby Mount Vesuvius made wines that were famous throughout Italy. But the mountain held a dark secret. In a gigantic eruption on August 24, Vesuvius obliterated Pompeii.

Forgotten for 1,700 years
Pompeii disappeared under the ash and was later planted over with grapevines. Excavations only began in 1763, and most of the town has since been uncovered, along with 2,000 of its citizens, frozen in time. Today, Pompeii provides a unique insight into the Roman world.

A dog's death
Bodies buried in the ash rotted away, leaving hollow cavities. Filled with plaster, these reveal victims and their pets in perfect detail.

A sea change
Pompeii was originally built on the coast. The rock and ash ejected from Vesuvius filled up so much of the bay that the excavated town is now two miles from the shore. In Roman times, the population was about 20,000, but today, millions live in the shadow of the volcano.

Tokyo earthquake

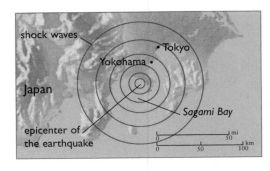

Sudden collapse
Measuring 8.2 on the Richter scale, the quake's epicenter was in Sagami Bay, where the seabed dropped by 1,300 feet. Near Tokyo, the thriving seaport of Yokohama was also almost completely destroyed.

Before September 1, 1923, Japan's capital was home to 2.5 million people. Then it was struck by one of the most devastating earthquakes in history. The main shock came at noon, when families were cooking lunch. Charcoal burners overturned, starting fires that spread rapidly among the closely packed wooden houses. Half the city burned and 142,000 people died. One million more, made homeless, moved away. Once the world's fifth-largest city, Tokyo became the tenth.

One million homeless

More than 500,000 of Tokyo's flimsy wooden houses collapsed or burned in the raging fires. Earth tremors, which continued for days, broke up the underground water pipes, making fire fighting impossible. People slept outside, afraid of being trapped under falling roofs. One eyewitness described the scene: "All day and all night, men, women, and children walk the camps and parks searching for lost relatives."

Danger below

Tokyo stands near a fault line, one of the meeting points of the moving, continent-sized plates that form the Earth's crust. As the plates grind together, they release shock waves that are felt on the surface as violent tremors.

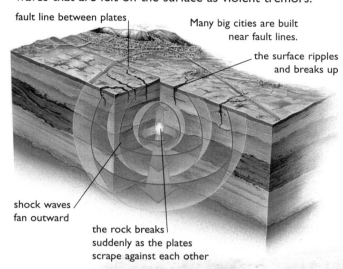

fault line between plates

Many big cities are built near fault lines.

the surface ripples and breaks up

shock waves fan outward

the rock breaks suddenly as the plates scrape against each other

An ever-present risk

Even with the latest construction methods, cities still face destruction today. The devastating 1995 earthquake at Kobe, 250 miles southwest of Tokyo, caused $10 billion in damage, killed 5,391 people, and left 310,000 homeless.

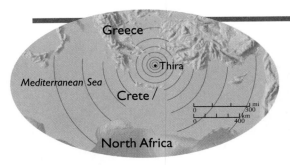

Coast to coast
An eruption on Thira, 70 miles to the north, caused the tsunami. Crete stood directly in the way of the huge waves that flooded coasts across the Mediterranean.

Tsunami

Imagine looking out to sea from a sunny beach. Something is wrong. The tide is going out—and not coming back. All the way to the horizon, the sea floor is revealed. Fish flop helplessly, boats are stranded. And then comes the huge wave. With a thunderous, deafening roar, it rears up like a moving mountain, crashing onshore with unimaginable force.

The drowning of an empire
The tsunami that struck the Mediterranean island of Crete around 1500 B.C. was one of the greatest natural disasters in history. The colossal 200-foot-high waves swept across the entire island, drowning the Minoan civilization—the oldest and richest in Europe. The destruction of this kingdom is the likely basis for the legend of the lost city of Atlantis.

Waves of destruction

The word *tsunami* comes from Japan, where "harbor waves" are a constant danger. The 30-foot-high giants that crashed into Okushiri Island on July 13, 1993 caused widespread devastation, killing more than 200 people.

Ocean racers

1. Undersea earthquakes and eruptions cause massive falls and rises in the ocean floor, convulsing the sea into great wave movements.

2. The waves, 600 miles or more wide, cause the entire sea level to rise. In open sea, they travel faster than a bullet speeding from a gun.

3. Near land, friction with the rising seabed slows the tsunami. The sea is sucked from the shore into the wave, making it rear up as it hits.

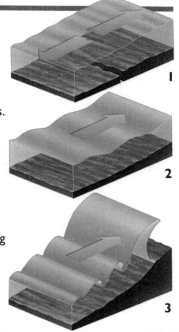

Frozen solid
Freezing rain is different from hail or snow. Each drop is a water-filled ice bomb, exploding on contact with a cold surface and freezing instantly into a hard, clear sheet of ice.

Ice storm

Canada is used to the cold, but the January 1998 storm caused a national emergency. Freezing rain clamped provinces such as Quebec and Ontario under a mantle of ice. Heat and lighting were cut off and the country's economy shut down, as millions were stranded in their freezing homes. Over 11,000 troops were mobilized to help restore power—the biggest military call-up in Canada's peacetime history.

Ice can build up dangerously on the wings of airplanes flying through clouds of freezing rain.

The only safe place is indoors, although damaged transmission towers may lead to power cuts.

Freezing rain forms a glaze on sidewalks, making them too slippery to walk on.

Roads covered by thick ice can be impossible to drive on.

Trees and electric transmission towers, coated with layers of ice, collapse under the enormous weight.

Cars and machinery left exposed are soon frozen solid.

Thick coat
Water falling as freezing rain turns to ice on impact. It can quickly build up to thicknesses of 4 inches, damaging property and killing farm livestock in minutes. Insured losses in Canada's freeze came to a massive $1.2 billion.

Deadly hazards of ice
Only a few people were found frozen to death after the storm, but many more died from carbon monoxide poisoning as they tried to keep warm with poorly ventilated homemade heaters created from barbecues. More were later reported killed by falling icicles during the thaw.

Toppled by the weight
Layers of ice enlarge electricity cables
to three times their usual width, dragging
down the steel towers supporting them.
At Drummondsville, south of Montreal,
a series of eight giant towers collapsed,
blacking out 482,000 homes in the city.
The ice storm raged for six days, but
it took weeks to restore power to the
millions left freezing in unlit houses
at temperatures as low as -17°F.

Twister

It emerged from thunderclouds over the state of Missouri, at 1 o'clock on March 18, 1925. Over the next three hours, the longest-lasting and most destructive tornado in history plowed through 10 towns. At times almost one mile wide and faster than a speeding car, the twister smashed thousands of homes and killed 689 people.

debris flung into the air is a major cause of casualties

homes in tornado black spots often have storm cellars for shelter

houses burst apart

wind speeds can exceed 300 feet per second

Brewing up a storm

Tornadoes are violent thunderstorms, caused when warm, wet air is drawn up from the ground and meets colder air moving down. The opposing drafts combine in a corkscrew motion, sending a violently spinning funnel of air plunging down to the ground.

Merciless killer

The most powerful twisters smash and grab everything in their way. Buildings, vehicles, and even the ground are sucked up into their vortices. The bodies of people caught up in the 1925 storm were hurled one mile from its path.

Missouri · Illinois · Indiana · Griffin · Princeton · Murphysboro · West Frankfort · Annapolis · Gorham · Ellington · path of tornado

Trail of devastation

The 1925 tornado raced 200 miles across the U.S.A.

- Appearing at Ellington, Missouri at 1 P.M., it took 15 minutes to wreck nearby Annapolis.

- Traveling northeast at 60 mph, it ripped into Illinois.

- In Murphysboro, 234 people died and 40 percent of the town was destroyed.

- The tornado subsided at 4:30 P.M., after hitting Princeton, Indiana.

Torn apart

Buildings in the path of a tornado often look as if they have exploded. Twisters tear at solid structures like a pair of giant hands wrenching savagely in opposite directions.

17

Bushfire

On December 2, 1997, Australia's largest city faced catastrophe. Fires raging in the bushland on three sides of Sydney suddenly swept into the suburbs. Before firefighters could gain control, dozens of houses were destroyed. The flames, whipped up by high winds, lit up the night sky as 5,000 emergency workers battled hundreds of separate fires. Only their courage, and a sudden change in the weather, prevented an even worse disaster.

Spreads like wildfire

In Australia's tinder-dry bush, fires are easily started—by lightning, arson, or even by the sun's rays magnified through the glass of a carelessly discarded bottle. Blazes spread at speeds of up to 1 mile a *minute*. The fires spread to within 12 miles of downtown Sydney, leaving the city darkened by choking smoke and fumes. Many homes were evacuated until the danger was past.

Street in flames
As Australia's fast-growing cities expand farther into the surrounding countryside, the danger from bushfires increases. The 1997 blaze burned out most of this street in the Sydney suburb of Menai.

Fighting fire with fire
Firebreaks help to stop the spread of a blaze in a forest. All the trees are felled and bulldozers clear the wood to the side of the break nearest the approaching flames. This material is then set alight to widen the firebreak.

Bombing the blazes
Bush and forest fires can be fought from the air. Highly skilled pilots skim the airplane over open water, scooping tons of it up into special tanks in the fuselage. The load is then released, like a bomb, onto the fire below.

Epidemic

Scientists now describe the influenza virus of 1918 as "the deadliest killer in human history." In six months it killed between 20 and 40 million people in a global epidemic—a pandemic—and then vanished. Unlike bubonic plague (the Black Death), which can be controlled by modern medicine, the flu has no known cure. If a similar virus broke out again, it could be the greatest disaster ever to strike humankind.

Flimsy protection

In 1918, people did not know how the deadly flu spread. Millions wore masks in the hope of avoiding infection when out in public places, but the gauze offered little protection against the microscopic virus.

Worsened by war

The virus struck toward the end of World War I (1914–18), killing twice as many people as the war itself. It was first called "Spanish flu," although it probably started in China. It reached Europe from the United States, carried by American servicemen on crowded troopships. In the filthy, wet trenches of the war zones, it spread like wildfire, mostly attacking young adults and causing death from lung infection, often within hours.

Hopeless cases

Emergency hospitals were set up to isolate patients in the hope of limiting the flu's spread. But there was no effective treatment, and victims who developed pneumonia as a complication were likely to die, literally drowning from the fluid filling their lungs. The antibiotics now used to combat pneumonia were not discovered until 1933. The spread of the virus could not be controlled either—ships carried it to every part of the globe, and by early 1919, nearly half of the world's 1.8 billion people had been infected.

A plague's progress

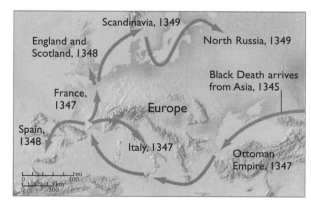

Scandinavia, 1349

England and
Scotland, 1348

North Russia, 1349

Black Death arrives
from Asia, 1345

France,
1347

Europe

Spain,
1348

Italy, 1347

Ottoman
Empire, 1347

The Black Death of 1347–52 spread to Europe from
the East. Carried by rats and transmitted to humans
by fleas, the plague killed about 25 million people,
reducing the population of some countries by a third.

Grim reaper

The bubonic plague, or
"Black Death", was a horrific
and deadly bacterial disease.
Its name came from the black,
blood-filled swellings visible
under victims' skin. So many
people died that carts piled
with corpses were a common
sight in towns and villages.
Many medieval people saw the
plague as a punishment from
God. Paintings of the time
depict Death as a skeleton
riding a cart over the bodies
of victims, rich and poor alike.

Locust

The swarm is vast. It blocks out the Sun. As many as 50 billion ravenously hungry insects are on the move. As the sinister black cloud, 30 miles long, passes over green fields, it suddenly wheels and descends with the deafening beat of countless wings. Minutes later, thousands of tons of crops have been devoured. All across Africa, in the summer of 1988, people faced famine because of an old enemy—the locust plague.

Danger in numbers
The African migratory locust is only 2 inches long, but in its adult, winged state it can fly up to 3,000 miles between breeding cycles. Each time the swarm feeds, females lay hundreds of eggs, increasing the number of locusts 100 times or more.

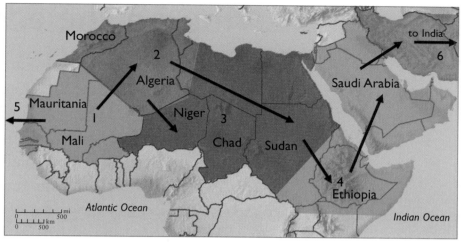

1. The wet winter of 1987–88 in Mali and Mauritania was ideal for locust breeding.

2. Early in 1988, the swarms moved north to devour crops in Morocco and Algeria.

3. By June, the swarm had eaten 1 million tons of crops in Chad, Niger, and Sudan.

4. Swarms then spread southeast to Ethiopia, reaching Saudi Arabia in the fall of 1988.

5. In October, a swarm was blown 3,000 miles across the Atlantic, a record flight of 5 days.

6. In 1989, a swarm of locusts reached India, almost 6,000 miles from the first breeding area.

Halfway around the world
In 1988, North Africa enjoyed exceptionally good crops of vital grains such as corn. But the wet weather was also ideal for locusts. Swarms were blown by prevailing winds right across the continent. Some even spread across the Atlantic and to India.

Alone in the desert
In the dry conditions usual in Africa, locusts are solitary creatures. They live like ordinary grasshoppers and are a dull, sandy color, which camouflages them from predators in the desert.

On the march
If rain comes, locusts feast on the fresh greenery and breed rapidly. The young become brightly colored to identify each other as they crowd together, hopping many miles to feed.

Ready for takeoff
If the weather stays wet and food remains plentiful, the locusts mature into their adult, winged form. They continue breeding and soon the first large swarms fly off to hunt for food.

A perpetual menace
Modern pesticides have done little to reduce the threat of locusts. The 1988 swarms, the most ruinous in 30 years, spread across half of Africa, even though the United Nations spent $240 million on spraying. The best control method is to treat locusts while they are immature "hoppers," foraging in large numbers on the ground. Once in flight, swarms can only be attacked from airplanes, which spray the insects from above.

Biting back
For thousands of years, locusts have provided a plentiful source of food for birds, animals—and humans. These people in Morocco have collected a large harvest, ready to be fried or grilled, and eaten like shrimp. Delicious!

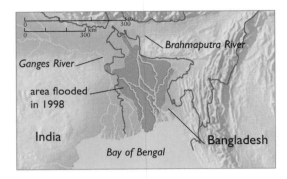

A nation under water

Bangladesh's population has grown from 80 million to 120 million since gaining independence in 1971. Most people live in the floodplains and deltas of the Ganges and Brahmaputra rivers, where fertile soil means good harvests, but floods regularly cover half the country.

Living on the edge

More than half the people on Earth live in places where floods are a constant danger. It's not as crazy as it sounds, because land that is regularly flooded by rivers is particularly fertile for farming. But the price can be terrible. The floodplains of the Ganges River in Bangladesh and the Yangtze River in China are two of the world's most heavily populated areas. In 1998, over two thirds of Bangladesh was submerged and 10 million people lost their homes. Calamity also struck China, where the Yangtze stranded millions more.

levees are built higher
as the river level rises

land is formed by mud
deposits left by floods

farmers prosper from
the rich soil's harvest

as the river drops sediment,
its bed becomes much higher
than the surrounding land

The gift of the river

Over thousands of years, rivers like the Yangtze in China have created fertile farmland, leaving layers of rich silt behind as they flood and then retreat. To protect their fields from severe flooding, farmers build giant levees of earth. These are reinforced by long nets woven from local crops and filled with stones.

In the breach

Levees have guarded China's farmland for centuries, and are often big enough to have roads along their tops. But sudden increases in water levels can cause disaster. After months of rain in 1998, the Yangtze burst through. More than 700,000 rescuers, including thousands of soldiers, struggled to reinforce the levees—but over one million people lost their homes.

From feast to famine

Living in a flood zone is a balancing act. The fertile land enables farmers to reap two or three harvests per year. But in disasters such as the Bangladesh floods of 1998, families face cruel hardships when rivers overflow. Their homes and fields are flooded, drowning the crops and leaving them buried under a new layer of mud. Then they are faced with months of food and medical shortages before the waters finally subside.

MAN-MADE DISASTERS

Alaskan coast
Oil spill, 1989

North Atlantic
Titanic, 1912

New York City
Wall Street crash, 1929

The disasters we bring upon ourselves are caused by human error, incompetence, and misfortune. Often they arise from a mixture of these—the famous sinking of *Titanic*, for example, is a story of too much confidence and sheer bad luck. Other cases stem from a series of small mishaps, none seemingly important on their own. The terrible air crash in Tenerife happened because mistake piled onto mistake until disaster struck.

The worst disasters, on the other hand, happen when clear warnings are ignored—as they were when operators shut down safety systems at the Chernobyl nuclear reactor. Engineers knew it was dangerous, but they

Tragedies of our own making
Triumphs of human technology
allow construction of great cities, fast
transportation, and powerful machines. Yet
with every achievement, there is the potential
for calamity if people grow careless or luck
runs out. This map shows some of the most
notable man-made disasters, which are
featured in this section.

Ireland
Famine,
1845

London, England
Bridge fire, 1212
Smog, 1952

Chernobyl, Ukraine
Nuclear explosion, 1986

Italian Alps
Landslide, 1963

Tenerife
Air crash, 1977

But man-made disasters have costs
that are not always measured in loss
of human life. The Wall Street Crash
killed no one, but led to a worldwide
depression in which tens of millions
lost their livelihoods. Increasingly
significant are environmental
catastrophes. The *Exxon Valdez* oil
spill and the Great London Smog are
only two examples of the devastation
that has been wrought worldwide
by humankind's carelessness with
modern resources.

carried on because they were used to
obeying orders. The tragedy was that
no one had the courage to say no to
the experiment before it was too late.

Thankfully, such major calamities are
rare events. In some areas, things are
actually getting safer—the number of
people killed each year in airplane
accidents has not risen since the
1950s, even though there are
now over one billion passenger
journeys taken every year.

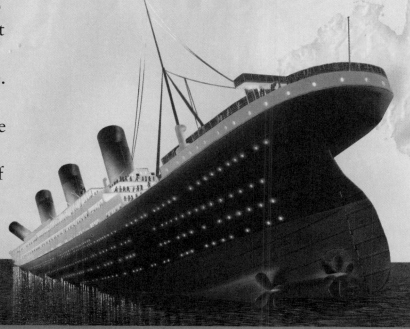

Famine

It was a national tragedy. By the 1840s, half the people of Ireland depended on just one food—the potato. It gave them most of the nutrients they needed, and many had stopped planting any other crop. Then, without warning, a new disease infected the potato plants, wiping out the harvest for years. In the famine that followed, one million Irish people died of starvation and sickness.

Grim harvest

Potato blight turned the crop into a black, foul-smelling slime. The disease, like the potato itself, came from America, arriving in Ireland in the summer of 1845. It spread rapidly, until Ireland's reliance on this single "miracle" crop—one man could plant enough plants to feed 40 people for a year—became a disaster.

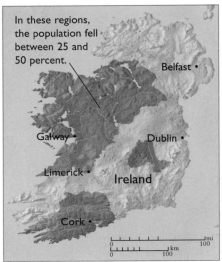

In these regions, the population fell between 25 and 50 percent.

Belfast •

Galway •

Dublin •

Limerick •

Ireland

Cork •

0 ——— 100 mi
0 ——— 100 km

Blighted land

In the three generations from 1785 to 1845, the Irish population had grown by three times, rising from 2.8 to 8.3 million. When the blight struck, millions died or emigrated, and the population plummeted. Even after the famine ended, poverty forced people to leave. Today, Ireland is home to only 4 million people.

Perilous crossing

Driven from the land, 1.2 million Irish people emigrated between 1847 and 1852, most to the United States. The long voyage in crowded, unsanitary ships was a dangerous one—about 16 out of every 100 passengers died at sea.

Help from above

Today, famine continues to plague many countries, especially in Africa, where food shortages due to crop failure can turn into disaster because of warfare or corruption. Then, international agencies must bring in emergency food by every means available.

Uncharitable response

Ireland, then a province of the United Kingdom,
was largely owned by English landlords, some of
whom reacted to the famine by throwing tenants off
their land when they could not pay the rent. People
who refused to leave were evicted by the army, who
often burned their homes to ensure that they would
not return. The British government did provide some
aid to Ireland—but it was too little, and too late.

Chernobyl

In April 1986, the world held its breath. Live television pictures from the Soviet Union showed that there had been an explosion at the Chernobyl nuclear power plant. A reactor, burning out of control, was belching tons of radioactive materials into the air. Soviet officials admitted to 31 deaths, but evacuated 135,000 people. Unknown numbers have since died from radiation sickness.

Raining uranium
During what the Soviet authorities called "an unauthorized experiment" by staff, Reactor No. 4 exploded at 1:23 A.M. on April 26. White-hot radioactive fuel fragments landed all over the power plant, starting fires near other reactors. Local firefighters risked their lives to enter the area and put out the flames.

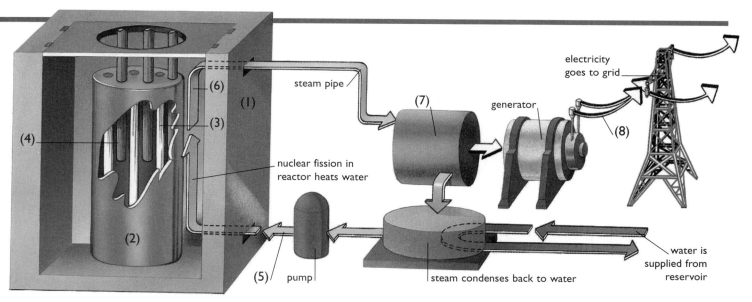

electricity goes to grid

steam pipe

(7)

generator

(8)

nuclear fission in reactor heats water

(6)

(1)

(3)

(4)

(2)

(5) pump

steam condenses back to water

water is supplied from reservoir

How a reactor works

Nuclear reactors harness heat energy produced by fission, the violent splitting of uranium atoms. The heat is used to generate electricity. Inside a concrete vessel (1), the reactor core (2) contains uranium fuel rods (3) and control rods (4), which are raised and lowered to control the rate of fission.

To cool the reactor, cold water is pumped in (5) and the reactor's heat turns the water to steam (6). The steam turns a turbine (7) to generate electricity (8). At Chernobyl, operators cut off the steam to see if the turbine would turn on its own. But it slowed immediately, reducing power to the water pumps that cools the reactor, which overheated instantly and violently.

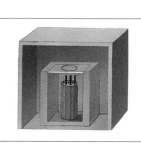 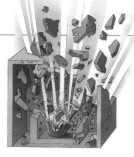 

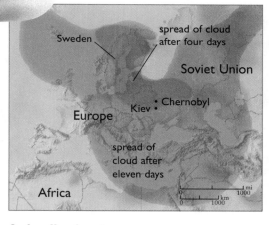

spread of cloud after four days

Sweden

Soviet Union

Kiev • Chernobyl

Europe

spread of cloud after eleven days

Africa

Bad vibrations

In seconds, the heat of the reactor had reached dangerous levels. But its automatic cooling system had been shut off and the control rods had been pulled up to increase power. Strong vibrations now made it impossible to lower the rods to cool the reactor.

Reaction force

The uncontrolled increase in reactor output began to melt the fuel rods. Uranium leaked into the cooling water, creating high-pressure steam and gases. These exploded, blowing the 2,000-ton roof off the reactor and out through the main building. The second explosion followed as the outside air came into contact with the reactor core.

Slow burner

The core burned for two weeks, sending tons of radioactive ash and dust into the outside air.

A deadly cloud

The first fallout was detected in Sweden on April 28. Winds and rain carried the dust cloud over Europe, contaminating farm produce for years. The Chernobyl reactor was finally buried under 5,000 tons of clay and sand, and sealed in a concrete tomb.

Cleaning action

Radioactive dust fell thickly on towns near the reactor, including Kiev, 75 miles away, where the streets had to be hosed down. In Chernobyl, trees were cut down, but could not be burned in case the smoke carried the poison back into the air. Everything was eventually buried in deep, concrete-lined pits.

Bridge on fire

On a blustery day in July 1212, fires broke out at both ends of London Bridge. Sweeping through the thatched buildings that lined the bridge, the flames trapped the crowds crossing the bridge. In the panic, about 3,000 people were burned or crushed to death, or drowned in the Thames River below. The fire spread, and most of the city was destroyed in a disaster far worse than London's Great Fire of 1666—in which only six lives were lost.

Fighting force
In cities today, dedicated firefighters can control even the most serious blaze. But it was only in the 19th century that the first full-time fire departments were established. By then, many of the world's cities, including New York, Rome, and Moscow, had been largely destroyed by fire at least once.

Demolition gangs

In the Middle Ages, there were no water hoses, so water could only be carried in buckets. To prevent the spread of fire between streets, some timber-framed houses were pulled down by teams using hooks attached to long poles and chains. This created a big gap across which the flames could not leap.

Safety measures

After the 1212 disaster, London introduced its first fire-prevention laws. Roofs thatched with highly flammable straw or rushes were banned in favor of stone tiles, and every district had to have its own set of hooks for pulling down buildings in an emergency.

Spanning the centuries

Built in the 1170s, the 1,000-foot London Bridge was home to hundreds of families. It was a shopping street as well as a vital thoroughfare, with a drawbridge and gatehouse at either end and a chapel in the middle. Although the houses were all destroyed in 1212, the stone piers survived and the bridge remained an important crossing for another 600 years.

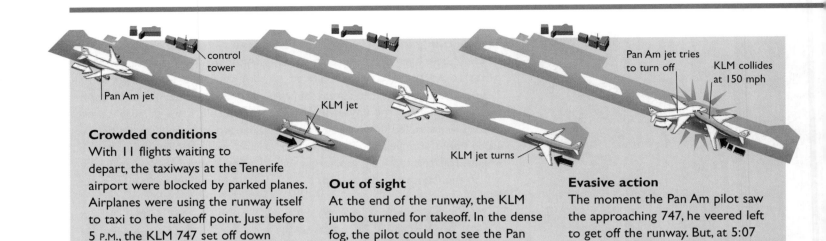

Crowded conditions
With 11 flights waiting to depart, the taxiways at the Tenerife airport were blocked by parked planes. Airplanes were using the runway itself to taxi to the takeoff point. Just before 5 P.M., the KLM 747 set off down the runway for the starting position, followed by the Pan Am jet.

Out of sight
At the end of the runway, the KLM jumbo turned for takeoff. In the dense fog, the pilot could not see the Pan Am jet straight ahead. He mistakenly believed he had permission to take off.

Evasive action
The moment the Pan Am pilot saw the approaching 747, he veered left to get off the runway. But, at 5:07 P.M., as the KLM jet left the ground, it crashed into the Pan Am's side.

Runway collision

The world's worst air disaster happened on the ground. On March 27, 1977, the fogbound airport on the Spanish island of Tenerife was busy with flights diverted by a terrorist bomb blast in nearby Las Palmas. In a series of misunderstandings between the control tower and the crews of two jets—a Dutch KLM and an American Pan Am—the two airplanes collided on the runway, killing 583 people.

Flying blind
The Pan Am pilot recalled, "We saw lights ahead of us in the fog. At first we thought it was the KLM standing at the end of the runway. Then we realized they were coming toward us." Only just airborne, the Dutch plane plowed into the Pan Am jet, then plunged to earth, where it exploded into flames.

Few survivors

Not visible from the control tower in the fog, the KLM jumbo burned out completely, killing all 248 on board. The crash's only survivors were those who managed to escape the stricken Pan Am jet before it too was destroyed by fire. Of the 634 people on board the planes, all but 51 died.

Fatal misunderstanding

The KLM pilot may have misheard a vital radio message from the control tower. He was not given takeoff permission, but radio interference could have made the ground controller's instruction, "OK. Stand by for take off," sound like, "OK for take off." The lack of ground radar (now used in all major airports) meant controllers could not "see" that the two planes were on a collision course.

Titanic

It should never have happened. On the night of April 14, 1912, the captain of the world's largest luxury liner knew he was in dangerous waters. In spite of ice warnings from ships nearby in the Atlantic, the *Titanic* was sailing at close to top speed. At 11:40 P.M., ice was sighted dead ahead. The 46,000-ton ship smashed into the iceberg, buckling the plates of her hull so that the water poured in. In under three hours, she was gone, and more than 1,500 people with her.

Collision course

It was a calm, clear night, but the dark mass of the iceberg blended in with the black sea. As soon as the danger came into view, the lookouts in the crow's nest above the foredeck rang the warning bell and phoned the bridge, "Iceberg, right ahead!" But it was too late.

Minutes from the end

Lights still blazed when the liner, taller than a 10-story building, finally upended and broke in half. It was 2 A.M., just 75 minutes after the first lifeboat had been lowered half-empty. At that time, many passengers refused to believe that the ship could sink. Now all the boats were gone and more than 1,000 people remained on board. "We could see groups clinging in clusters or bunches, like swarming bees," recalled one survivor, "only to fall in masses, pairs, or singly as the great part of the ship rose into the sky."

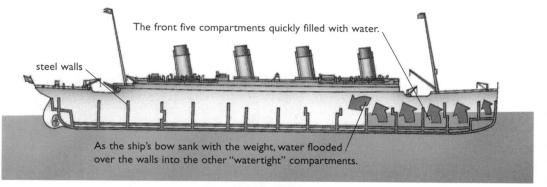

The front five compartments quickly filled with water.

steel walls

As the ship's bow sank with the weight, water flooded over the walls into the other "watertight" compartments.

Damage beyond control

Below decks, the *Titanic* was divided into compartments. If the hull was damaged, only one section would flood. But the iceberg ruptured five at once. As the weight of the seawater dragged down the liner's bow, the front of the hull rapidly flooded.

Wasted lives

The last lifeboat to be launched—seen here from the liner *Carpathia*, the first ship to the rescue—was almost full. But in the confusion, many lifeboats had been lowered with empty seats, costing as many as 500 people their chance of survival. Of 2,223 on board, only 492 passengers and 214 crew escaped.

Oil spill

A message came from the captain of the giant supertanker *Exxon Valdez*: "Evidently we are leaking some oil." His 200,000-ton ship had run aground only hours after taking on a full load at the oil terminal in Prince William Sound, Alaska. It was Good Friday, March 24, 1989. By Monday, 10 million gallons of crude oil had spilled into the sea. It was one of the worst environmental disasters in history.

Circling the spill
Because oil is lighter than water and floats on the surface, inflatable tubes called booms are used to prevent slicks from spreading. The boom is reeled out from a ship to trap the slick in a loop. The oil can then be pumped from the surface into tankers.

Human failing
The *Exxon Valdez* disaster was caused by a simple navigational error. After leaving the port of Valdez, the crew changed course to avoid floating ice. They then failed to resume the usual course and struck a reef. The captain was asleep at the time. Investigators later found out that he had been drinking and had entrusted the steering to an inexperienced helmsman.

Widespread pollution
Tides carried the spilled oil over 1,500 miles of Alaska's southern coastline, an area of great unspoiled beauty. Cleanup work was seriously delayed as companies and officials argued over who would have to pay for it.

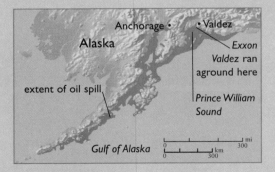

The cost to the region's wildlife was devastating. Ten years later, some species still had not recovered fully.

Many of the killer whale pods in Alaskan waters disappeared after the disaster.

Hundreds of cormorants were killed. Their populations have not yet recovered.

Mussels, an essential food for both birds and otters, were badly polluted by the spill.

Rare sea otters had been growing in number, but the oil spill killed thousands.

Salmon fishing was stopped to prevent the contaminated fish reaching stores.

Common seaweed, vital to all coastal ecosystems, was severely affected.

Helping hands
Volunteers flocked to Alaska to help with the huge task of rescuing oil-covered birds and animals. One good thing did come out of the disaster, after disputes over who should pay for the cleanup. The world's oil companies and shipowners agreed to the Valdez Principles, which will ensure they take responsibility for oil spills in the future.

The blackened shore

Cleaning up the *Exxon Valdez* spill took years and cost an incredible $20 billion. On shore, some teams used high-pressure hoses to dislodge the oil. Others simply shoveled it up from the beaches and carried it away in buckets. But oil clings like glue to everything it touches—especially fur and feathers. In Alaska, it killed at least 580,000 seabirds and 5,500 sea and river otters. The breeding grounds of countless seals, sea lions, fish, and birds were contaminated, and research into the long-term effects on Alaska's uniquely precious wildlife continues today.

Smog

It is a blend of smoke and fog, a choking mixture of man-made pollution and natural mist, which settles over cities with potentially fatal results. In London, England, then the world's largest city, the Great Smog of 1952 killed 4,000 people in four days—and twice that number died later from its effects. After years of ignoring the problem, the government was forced to introduce tough clean air laws. Despite the lessons learned, smog remains a serious hazard in cities across the world today.

Stacks of smoke
Fifty years ago, Western nations depended on coal fires and coal-burning power plants, which all emitted filthy smoke. Many fuels are now cleaner, but increased burning worldwide means that pollution continues.

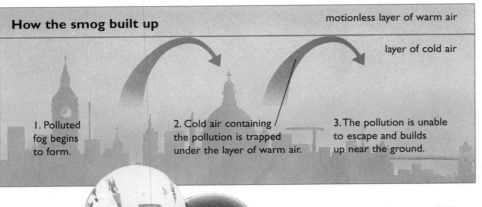

How the smog built up

motionless layer of warm air

layer of cold air

1. Polluted fog begins to form.

2. Cold air containing the pollution is trapped under the layer of warm air.

3. The pollution is unable to escape and builds up near the ground.

Cold trap
Built in the low-lying basin of the Thames River, London has always been prone to the fog that forms as warm air condenses over cold ground. On December 4, 1952, a "temperature inversion" occurred, when polluted cold air was trapped under a static layer of warm air. With no wind to shift it, the poisonous smog lingered until December 9 before finally clearing.

Not so clean air
City dwellers in the Far East now commonly wear protection against pollution. In the Malaysian capital Kuala Lumpur, smoke from forest fires has combined with industrial and traffic fumes to make the air so dangerous that police are issued masks. In the United States, cities like Los Angeles have levels of dangerous fumes 400 times higher than the Clean Air Act allows.

Thick as pea soup

At times during the Great Smog, visibility in London was less than three feet. Buses, ambulances, and fire engines had to be led through the streets by guides carrying flares, and people got lost just a few feet from their own homes. The air, laden with filthy carbon and sulfur dioxide, turned the yellow-green color that Londoners knew as "pea soup." Up to 10 times heavier than normal air, the smog was lethal to people with heart or lung problems.

Landslide

Spanning a steep river gorge in the Italian Alps, the Vaiont Dam was the second highest in the world—and the most dangerous. Rockfalls were common in the region, and experts warned that the reservoir created by the dam could cause the submerged mountainsides to collapse. But the project went ahead. On October 9, 1963, the worst happened. A huge avalanche plunged into the lake, sending millions of tons of water over the dam and into the heavily populated valley.

Like an earthquake

The landslide hit the reservoir's floor with an impact that was felt all over Europe. The mountainous movement generated a rush of air so violent that it lifted the roofs from houses for miles around, and blew out windows and doors. Incredibly, the dam survived, but the vast body of water that surged over its top formed a 230-foot-high wave which swept away everything in its path, leaving more than 2,000 people dead.

Moving mountain

At 10:41 P.M., a mile-wide strip of Mount Toc, the reservoir's south bank, collapsed. It filled half the lake, displacing 63.4 billion gallons of water. The torrent sent over the dam destroyed most of the town of Longarone and several villages. At the lake's east end, hundreds more homes were deluged by waves from the impact.

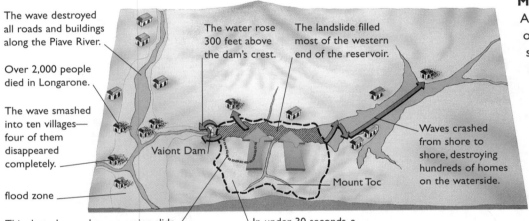

The wave destroyed all roads and buildings along the Piave River.

Over 2,000 people died in Longarone.

The wave smashed into ten villages—four of them disappeared completely.

flood zone

Vaiont Dam

The water rose 300 feet above the dam's crest.

The landslide filled most of the western end of the reservoir.

Mount Toc

Waves crashed from shore to shore, destroying hundreds of homes on the waterside.

This dotted area shows a major slide from just three years earlier, which the dam's builders had ignored.

In under 30 seconds, a gigantic section of Mount Toc plummeted into the reservoir.

After the event

A priest prays over a victim of the Vaiont Dam disaster. Many of the dead were unidentified, as no one nearby survived to name them. The dam, built to generate hydroelectricity, had been in full operation for only a few months, following years of delay due to doubts about possible danger from landslides.

Snowed under

Avalanches are a constant hazard in mountain ranges such as the Alps in central Europe. The risk of disastrous snowfalls increases in farming regions and ski resorts where mountainsides have been cleared of the trees that help to stabilize ground snow.

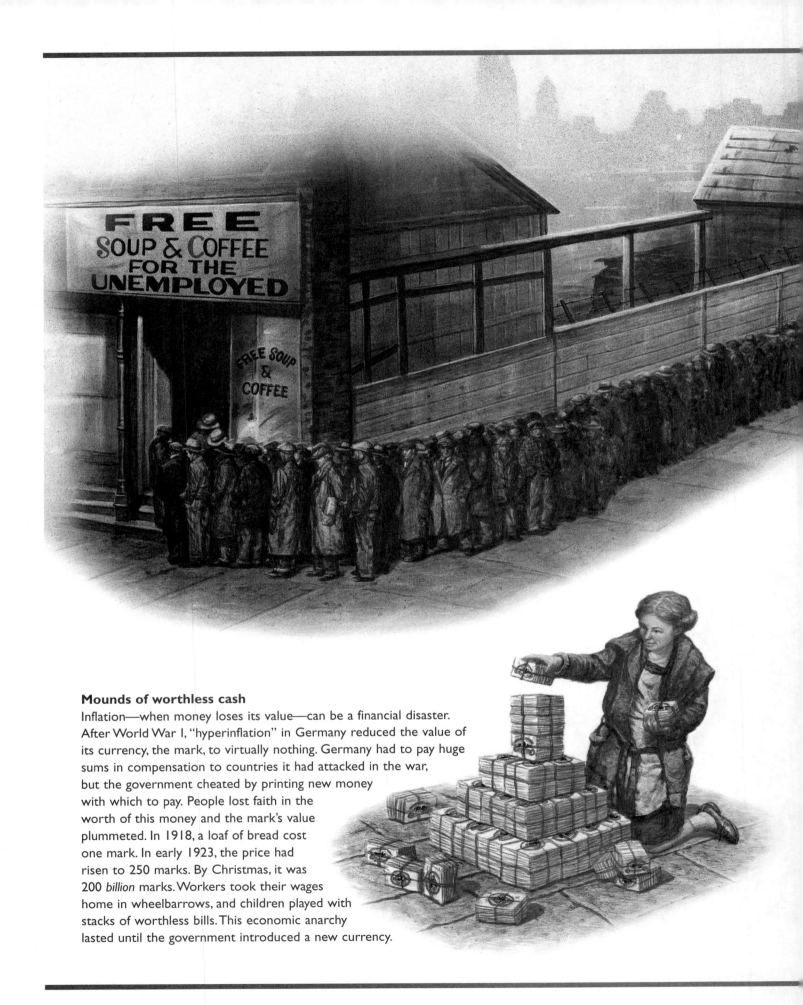

Mounds of worthless cash

Inflation—when money loses its value—can be a financial disaster. After World War I, "hyperinflation" in Germany reduced the value of its currency, the mark, to virtually nothing. Germany had to pay huge sums in compensation to countries it had attacked in the war, but the government cheated by printing new money with which to pay. People lost faith in the worth of this money and the mark's value plummeted. In 1918, a loaf of bread cost one mark. In early 1923, the price had risen to 250 marks. By Christmas, it was 200 *billion* marks. Workers took their wages home in wheelbarrows, and children played with stacks of worthless bills. This economic anarchy lasted until the government introduced a new currency.

FREE
SOUP & COFFEE
FOR THE
UNEMPLOYED

FREE SOUP & COFFEE

Wall Street crash

The peace and welfare of every nation depend on its economic security. But that security is not guaranteed. Financial disasters can create mass poverty—as happened in the United States after the stock market crash of October 24, 1929. Share prices fell so low that many companies became worthless. Investors lost their money and businesses went bankrupt. With the country engulfed by depression, millions lost their jobs, then their homes. They went on the road in search of work, dependent on charity for survival. Countless numbers died from starvation and illness.

Standing in line

As the Great Depression gripped the United States, the unemployment level soared to 14 million people and the average income was halved. Americans, receiving no welfare, relied on soup kitchens—or begging—to stay alive. Recovery only began after a new president, Franklin D. Roosevelt, introduced the New Deal in 1933. This helped the poor find food, shelter, and work through community projects—building roads, dams, and houses.

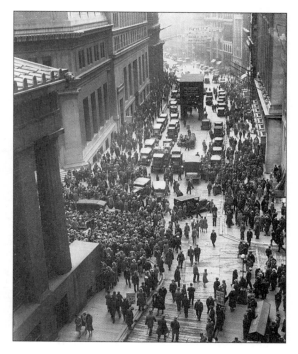

Hard times for farmers

In 1932, with the Depression at its height, America suffered another economic disaster. After years of good harvests from the great wheat-growing plains of the Midwest, the vast region was struck by a severe drought. The land soon became a "dust bowl." Farmers lost their properties and moved into crude shacks. Half a million people abandoned their land before the drought ended—five long years later.

Panic in the street

On the morning of the crash, the stock exchange on New York City's Wall Street was a scene of chaos. Large investors were selling shares in response to fears about the worldwide economy. As news of the falling prices spread, thousands of small investors ordered their stockbrokers to sell "at any price." Panic broke out as brokers failed to find any buyers. Millions of shares worth billions of dollars became entirely worthless in a matter of hours.

FUTURE DISASTERS

Is life on Earth becoming more dangerous? In one very important sense, it is. Our global population is now 100 times greater than 500 years ago, and it is increasing at a frightening rate. Millions more people are now exposed to natural disasters, and the upsurge in population puts pressure on people's quality of life across the globe. Many cities now face poverty, epidemics, overcrowding, and rising crime.

Meanwhile, human technology causes increasing damage to Earth's environment. By stripping away the forests that once covered much of the land, and by polluting the atmosphere with industrial waste and transport fumes, we have set in motion the process of global warming. This has already led to an increase in violent weather and flooding—and the risk that the ice caps could melt, drowning much of the world.

Technology has made our lives safer. New medicines can combat diseases that were once untreatable. But a final triumph over illness is a long way off. Some diseases can be controlled, but none is eradicated.

Another threat comes from space. Giant meteorites have struck Earth before, and sooner or later another will appear. We can only trust that when this happens, our ingenuity will be able to prevent catastrophe.

Getting hotter

Think of the world as a greenhouse. The glass walls and roof are the Earth's atmosphere, letting in the sunlight and trapping the heat to keep the inside warm. But there's a growing problem. Gases from fuels burned off by industry, transportation, and deforestation are building up in the atmosphere, so that heat is escaping more slowly. This greenhouse effect is causing global warming—already a cause for alarm.

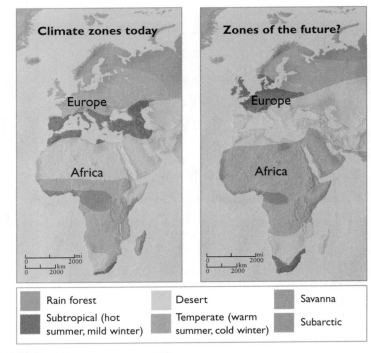

Climate zones today

Zones of the future?

Europe

Africa

Europe

Africa

Rain forest	Desert	Savanna
Subtropical (hot summer, mild winter)	Temperate (warm summer, cold winter)	Subarctic

Long-range forecast

If global warming continues, the polar ice caps could melt and climate zones around the world will move northward. In the latitudes of Europe, for example, cool countries such as France, Germany, and Britain would become subtropical. Sunny Spain and Italy would be scorched into deserts, and hot, dry North Africa would turn into a vast expanse of grassy savanna.

Paris in the heat

In the future, could northern cities such as Paris be sweltering in subtropical weather? Yes, say some experts, if global warming causes a shift in world climate belts. While northern regions might welcome warmer weather, the possible effects on agriculture could be calamitous. The world's grain-growing regions could turn into deserts, leading to mass famine. Global warming could make changes to rainfall patterns, too. Regions with regular rain year-round may soon face monsoonlike downpours that cause disastrous floods. If nothing else, the world will begin to look very different. The pyramids of Egypt, for example, would no longer stand in dry desert sands, but in green grasslands.

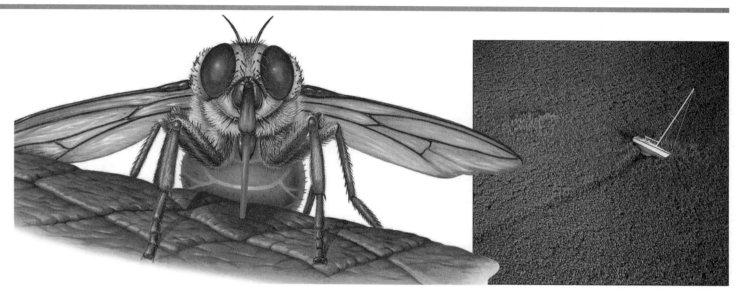

Unwelcome visitors

Temperatures may increase by up to five degrees Fahrenheit during the next 100 years—five times more than the last. This would enable warm-climate plant and wildlife species to migrate north, perhaps bringing unwelcome visitors, such as the deadly tsetse fly and malarial mosquito, to parts of Europe and the United States where these insects have never been a threat before.

Building up a storm

Global warming is blamed for an increase in the number of violent storms. Hurricanes such as Mitch, which devastated Central America in 1998, are said to have become 40 percent more frequent since 1970.

World under water

If our planet continues to warm up, we could all be in serious trouble. Water expands as it heats, so the oceans would rise and threaten coastlines. There is a danger, too, that the polar ice caps may gradually melt as temperatures increase. Some scientists predict that the combined effect could cause a catastrophic rise in sea levels by the end of the 21st century. Without flood defenses in place, major cities would be at risk in many heavily populated regions of the world.

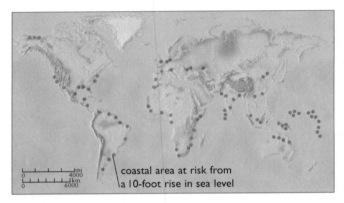

coastal area at risk from a 10-foot rise in sea level

Disappearing from the map

Some scientists have estimated that sea levels could rise 10 feet by the year 2100. If this happens, dozens of coastal belts, including major cities such as Bangkok, St. Petersburg, and New Orleans would face disastrous flooding. Whole regions including southern Florida, much of the Netherlands, and half of Bangladesh would be awash. The areas at risk account for one third of the world's vital crop-growing land.

Wet outlook

The prospect of coastal cities such as New York sheltering behind seawalls in centuries to come is real. In the last 100 years, the average sea level has risen by 4 to 10 inches, and the United Nations forecasts that it will rise four times faster in the 21st century. Ocean currents will cause much greater increases in some regions, threatening coastlines in future centuries with tides 10 to 16 feet higher than present levels, even without the extra hazard of melting polar ice caps.

Hole in the sky

Pollution causes more danger than global warming. Chemicals called CFCs—used, for example, in aerosols—drifted up into the sky for decades, destroying the ozone layer, the part of the Earth's atmosphere that protects us from cancer-causing ultraviolet sunlight. The risk was ignored, until a huge hole was detected in the ozone layer over Antarctica in 1987. CFCs are now controlled, but too late to prevent this grave environmental disaster.

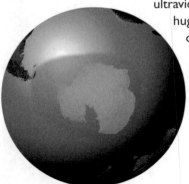

Against the tide
The Thames Barrier, completed in 1984, protects London, England from the dangerous high tides that began to flood the city in the 20th century. The main gates, which each weigh 3,700 tons, close into a wall as high as a five-story building. The barrier has had to be raised 33 times in its first 15 years.

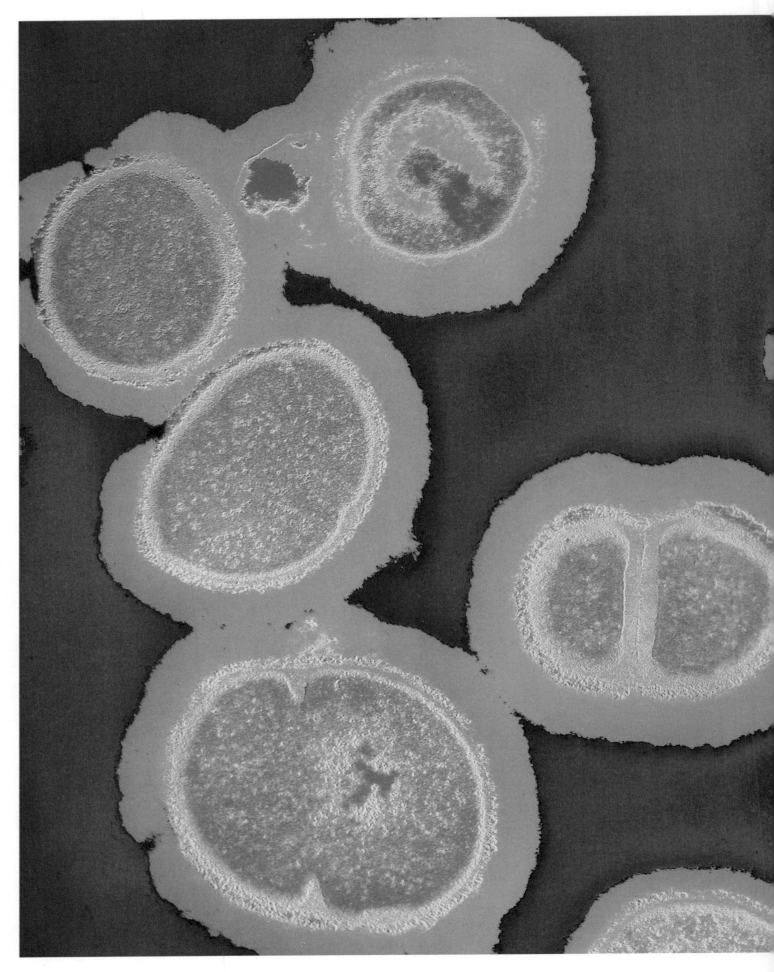

Medical threats

Our most dangerous enemies are invisible. In spite of medicine's amazing progress in the 20th century, microscopic monsters continue to stalk us. Deadly new viral diseases such as AIDS and Ebola have no known cure so far. And infectious bacteria, responsible for killers such as diphtheria and tuberculosis, are also staging a comeback. They have begun to develop resistance to antibiotics, the miracle drugs that doctors once hoped would consign them to history.

Risky business
To find new treatments for infectious diseases, researchers test thousands of different chemicals, one by one, on samples of the bacteria that cause them. It is a time-consuming task and often a hazardous one. Testing deadly germs calls for extreme care and special precautions.

Survival expert

MRSA (Methicillin-resistant *Staphylococcus Aureus*) is a "superbug" which even powerful antibiotics cannot destroy. The bacterium lives in hospitals, where it attacks—and kills—patients who have had operations. Pictured (*left*) at 500,000 times its actual size, MRSA is so dangerous that some hospitals refuse to admit patients who have the infection. Scientists are developing drugs to combat MRSA, but these miniscule organisms learn to change their form and behavior just as quickly as new drugs appear. Their struggle to survive is as determined as that of any other life form.

Ancient remedy

In the search for cures, medicine turns to some surprising sources. A powerful new treatment for malaria, which kills millions each year, is based on a 2,000-year-old Chinese herbal remedy and taken from the common plant family *Artemisia*.

Persistent killer
New diseases pose a constant threat of disastrous epidemics. In Africa, millions live in fear of the Ebola virus, named after a deadly outbreak in the Ebola River region of Zaire in 1976. One sufferer was transferred to the capital, Kinshasa, where the disease was found to be new—and infectious enough to threaten the city's two million people. The hospital, and the Ebola region, were instantly sealed off. The fever kills up to 90 percent of its victims and cannot be cured. It broke out again in 1995, killing most of the staff and patients at a hospital in Kikwit, Zaire. The virus is so infectious that even burial parties must wear protective clothing.

Crowded planet

Thanks to 20th-century technology, we live longer, travel farther, and produce more goods. We also multiply. There are now six billion of us, four times as many as 100 years ago. We run one billion motor vehicles on our roads and consume more and more of the Earth's resources. In another century, there could be 15 billion people, all in need of jobs, homes, food, health care, and transportation. Unless growth slows, the world could be overwhelmed.

Population explosion

The United Nations hopes people will learn to limit children to two per couple. Population growth next century will depend on when this target is reached. The graph shows three possibilities. The highest figure is the likeliest, and could well be exceeded.

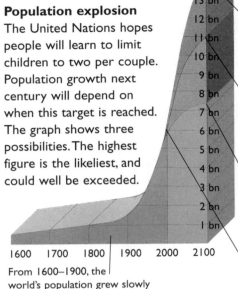

Two children per family not reached until 2065. World population is 14.2 billion in 2100.

Two children per family not reached until 2035. World population is 11 billion in 2100.

Two children per family reached by 2010. Population is 7.5 billion in 2100.

The world's population today is 6 billion.

From 1600–1900, the world's population grew slowly from 0.6 billion to 1.6 billion.

Key disadvantages
• Computers have revolutionized many activities, but our growing dependence on them may lead to problems in the future.
• Software "bugs" threaten vital systems such as air-traffic control and defense.
• Users are deskbound and can suffer from lack of personal contact.
• Children may become addicted to games, damaging their health and education.

Chaos in the streets

The city of the future is a crowded, nightmare vision. Dirty, traffic-choked streets and sidewalks are squeezed between high-rise buildings, in which solitary workers sit all day at computers in soundproof, sealed offices. Some cities are, of course, just like this now, but it is going to get much worse. Britain, for example, already has one of the world's most overcrowded road networks, with 100 vehicles for almost every mile. With car use growing at its present rate, there will be 50 percent more traffic by 2030. This dependence on cars will cause yet more problems of congestion, accidents, and pollution.

Throwaway society
European households each throw out a ton of trash every year. In the United States, it is even more. Disposal by burying or burning damages the environment—and the problem gets worse as people worldwide generate more and more waste.

Uncontrolled spread

Populations in the industrialized nations of Europe and North America are growing slowly, but in the developing world, high birthrates double some countries' numbers every 20 to 30 years. Millions flock to cities, hoping to share the benefits of the consumer society. The many who find no work face a grim life in shanty towns such as those of Rio de Janeiro in Brazil (*left*)—already overcrowded and beset by poverty and disease.

San Francisco earthquake

Had the founders of San Francisco been warned, back in 1776, that they were building in one of the most dangerous places on Earth, they might well have decided to go elsewhere. But no warnings came, and San Francisco grew into a large and flourishing city. Yet it is located almost directly above the San Andreas Fault, the unstable intersection of two moving plates in the Earth's crust, and today's inhabitants know they could be struck, at any time, by the kind of massive earthquake that destroyed the city in 1906.

Seconds from catastrophe

How much damage will a severe local earthquake do to San Francisco? The city had a disturbing foretaste in October 1989. An 11-second shock, only a tenth of the magnitude of the great 1906 quake, caused $6 billion in damage, made 12,000 people homeless, and toppled an elevated section of highway, killing 42 motorists. Had the earthquake lasted the normal 20 to 30 seconds, thousands more buildings and roads would have been destroyed.

Shaken but undeterred

Just after 5 A.M. on April 16, 1906, San Francisco's half-million people were shaken awake by a terrifying earthquake. Buildings and roads collapsed, but the main damage came from the fires, started by gas leaks, which ravaged the city for three days. More than 700 people died and most of the city was destroyed. Afterward, some citizens said it would be crazy to rebuild the city where it was sure to be struck again some day. But within three years, the central district had been completely restored—with new roads, bridges, and buildings, all capable of withstanding severe shock and resisting fire. The San Francisco Bay Area now has 10 times the population of a century ago.

shear walls reinforced with steel

central core has elevators and stairs

cross-bracing strengthens structure

steel frame needs no core

welded joints for increased strength

shock-resistant foundations are made of steel and rubber

Built to last

To prevent collapse during severe earthquakes, many modern buildings are cagelike structures formed around a strong central core. "Shear" (one-piece) reinforced concrete walls and outer walls "cross-braced" with diagonal beams provide support. Some buildings have steel frames welded into a single rigid structure—this needs less internal strengthening.

Well prepared

The town of Parkfield lies on the San Andreas Fault in a region of California hit by huge quakes in 1857 and 1983. It is now said to be the most intensely earthquake-monitored place in the world. The town's school is built to resist violent tremors, with shatterproof windows and all heavy items from bookcases to computers bolted down. Pupils have earthquake drills at least once a month.

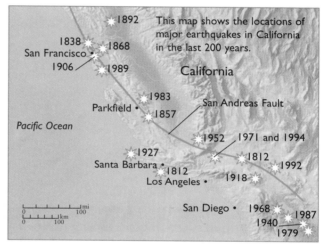

This map shows the locations of major earthquakes in California in the last 200 years.

1892

1838 — San Francisco • — 1868
1906 — 1989

California

1983
Parkfield • — 1857 — San Andreas Fault

Pacific Ocean

1952 — 1971 and 1994

1927
Santa Barbara • — 1812 — 1812 — 1992
Los Angeles • — 1918

San Diego • — 1968 — 1987
1940 — 1979

Danger zone

The San Andreas Fault, extending 750 miles through California, is the meeting point of two sections of the Earth's crust, the Pacific and North American plates. Earthquakes, caused by the plates grinding against each other, happen regularly here. There has been a major one about every 10 years for the last two centuries.

Meteorite!

Is bombardment from outer space pure science fiction? Not at all, according to scientists. The Earth is scarred by hundreds of impact sites. These include a crater carved by the meteorite probably responsible for the extinction of the dinosaurs 65 million years ago, and the vast area of Siberia obliterated by an exploding fireball as recently as 1908. No single death has been officially attributed to a space object—so far. How long will our luck hold?

Crash course

Asteroids, small planets orbiting the Sun, range from 600-mile-wide giants to tiny rock and iron fragments. When these objects hit Earth, we call them meteorites. The Earth collides harmlessly with small debris every day, nearly all of which is burned up in the atmosphere, but if a large object struck, it could lead to worldwide devastation. Scientists estimate the chances of impact with such a meteorite at once every million years. Even so, they now constantly monitor space, because it could come at any time. It is only a slight comfort that an incoming object could possibly be intercepted by nuclear weapons to keep it from colliding with Earth.

Big hole
The Meteor Crater in Arizona provides unmistakable evidence that a huge object crashed into the Earth 50,000 years ago. To create such a pit, almost a mile wide and 575 feet deep, the meteorite must have been 130 feet wide, weighing 300,000 tons, and traveling at more than 30,000 mph.

Wiped out
The sudden extinction of the dinosaurs 65 million years ago was probably the result of a massive meteorite strike. A 110-mile-wide crater recently found near Mexico's Yucatán Peninsula is believed to be the point of impact.

Big bang
Any meteorite large enough to enter our atmosphere without breaking up would hit the surface with a force greater than an atomic explosion. The shock would turn the surrounding land into dust. The impact of an object one mile or more across would incinerate everything for hundreds of miles around, sending ash and dust up into the atmosphere, darkening the world. Survivors of the blast and the giant waves caused by the shock might eventually die due to lack of sunlight.

shock wave

global darkness

greenhouse effect increases

falling debris

impact site

rock is vaporized

bushfires

tsunami

earthquakes

Glossary

AIDS Acquired Immune Deficiency Syndrome, a fatal illness caused by HIV (Human Immunodeficiency Virus). Sufferers lose resistance to infections.

antibiotics Drugs made to combat bacteria.

asteroid A small, rocky object orbiting the sun. Collisions between asteroids, or a large planet's gravitational pull, cause some to change orbit and collide with Earth.

Atlantis In ancient Greek legend, a great civilization that was lost under the sea.

bacteria Single-celled organisms, some of which cause infectious diseases. Most can be controlled with antibiotics.

bubonic plague An infectious bacterial disease, named after the "buboes" (swellings) under victims' skin. Also called the Black Death.

bushfire Fires in open country, often caused by drought, lightning strikes, or arson.

carbon The element in fossil fuels, such as coal or oil, that gives off heat energy when burned.

carbon monoxide Poisonous gas given off by the burning of fossil fuels, such as coal or oil, to generate heat or power.

CFCs Chlorofluorocarbons, the gases used in aerosols and fridges. The release of CFCs into the air causes destructive chemical reactions in the ozone layer.

delta The coastal region where a great river approaches the sea. The area's land is formed of fertile silt.

diphtheria An infectious bacterial disease affecting the throat. It makes breathing and swallowing very difficult.

ecosystem A community of living organisms. Each part of the system depends on others, and destruction of any single part of the system affects the rest.

epicenter The point on the Earth's surface directly above the source of an earthquake.

fault line The place where the mobile plates that make up the Earth's surface meet.

firebreak In fire fighting, a space created by clearing away vegetation or buildings. The fire cannot cross this gap.

fission In nuclear physics, the splitting of the component parts of atoms to produce energy.

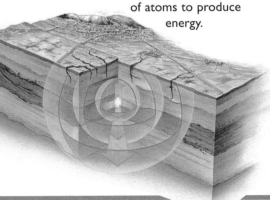

fissure A crack in the ground caused by an earthquake or by volcanic activity.

floodplain The low-lying area around a river or along a coastline where flooding is common.

greenhouse effect The heating of the Earth's atmosphere by pollution from burning fuels. The atmosphere naturally holds in the sun's life-giving heat, but pollution prevents the heat from escaping as quickly as before. This causes world temperatures to increase—the process of "global warming."

hoppers In the locust life cycle, young insects with well-developed legs, but without wings.

hydroelectricity Electricity produced by water rushing from a dam's channels to turn turbines in a power plant.

inflation The loss of money's value. If prices rise so that an item priced at $1 in January costs $1.10 in December, inflation is 10 percent. If the price rises from $1 to, say, $100 or more, that is hyperinflation.

latitude On a map, the distance north or south from the equator. Thus, New York, Madrid, Rome, and Beijing are on approximately the same latitude.

lava Molten rock that pours from a volcano in an eruption.

levee A long, continuous mound raised on either side of a river to contain flooding.

magma The superhot layer of liquid rock in the Earth's crust.

meteorite A fragment of an asteroid that penetrates the Earth's atmosphere and collides with the surface.

Minoan civilization An early culture on the island of Crete.

monsoon A seasonal wind in southern Asia that brings torrential rains each year.

nuclear power The harnessing of nuclear fission to generate electricity.

nutrients The substances in foods that provide nourishment.

ozone A gas in the atmosphere that absorbs a lot of the ultraviolet light from the sun's rays.

pandemic A disease epidemic that spreads around the world.

plates Huge moving sections of the Earth's crust that lie beneath continents and oceans.

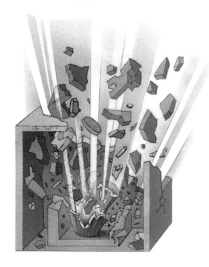

potato blight A destructive and fast-spreading disease caused by fungus. It breaks down potatoes into a salty mush.

pyroclastic flow A dense cloud of burning rock, ash, and gases that rolls down the sides of some erupting volcanoes at enormous speeds.

radioactive Atomic materials such as uranium exist in a constant state of nuclear disintegration and consequently emit radioactivity, which is fatal in large doses.

seismic Relating to earthquakes.

shares To raise money in order to expand their businesses, major companies issue shares. Each share represents a proportion of the company's value. Investors buy the shares in the hope that they will increase in value.

shock wave A sudden, violent change in air pressure caused by an explosion, earthquake, or massive movement such as a landslide.

silt The loose sand and earth carried by rivers and deposited across floodplains.

stockbroker A person whose job is to buy and sell shares for people who invest in the world's stock markets.

stock market Most large companies are publicly owned, which means that their shares can be bought by anyone on what is called the stock market. To buy or sell shares, investors use the stock exchanges that have been established in most nations.

sulfur dioxide A poisonous gas produced by burning fuels.

tornado Violent winds that whirl in a funnel-shaped formation.

tsunami Giant sea waves caused by undersea earthquakes or volcanoes.

tuberculosis A bacterial disease of the lungs.

turbine A propeller-like engine turned by water, steam, gas, or wind to generate electricity.

ultraviolet Hazardous radiation in sunlight. It is filtered by the ozone layer.

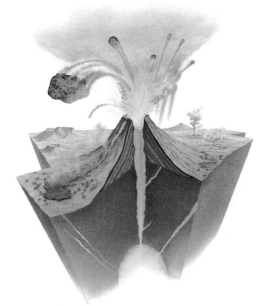

United Nations An association of all the world's recognized nations, dedicated to maintaining peace and human welfare.

uranium A mineral element used as a source of nuclear energy.

virus A microscopic organism that survives by invading a host animal or human. It causes disease as it multiplies in the body. Viruses cannot by killed by antibiotics.

vortex The spinning effect of rapidly circulating air that forms a tornado.

Index

Acknowledgments

The publishers would like to thank the following
illustrators for their contributions to this book:

b = bottom, c = center, l = left, r = right, t = top, m = middle

Marion Appleton 5 *tr;* **T James Bayley** 2 *tr,* 19 *tl,* 26 *bl,* 27 *br,* 30, 35 *tr,* 36–37 *b,* 38 *ml,* 40 *cl,* 42 *bl,* 53 *tr,*
54 *bl, cl,* 56, 62 *tr;* **Julian Baum** 46 *t,* 62 *tl;* **Stephen Conlin** 7 *bl;* **Richard Draper** 3 *tl,* 14 *m,* 17 *tr,* 23 *m,*
25 *t,* 28 *bl,* 31 *t, c,* 34 *t,* 36 *tl,* 37 *t,* 42 *c,* 54 *t,* 57 *cl,* 59 *br,* 60 *tr,* 61 *tc, bl;* **David Farren** 2 *bl,* 15, 19 *b,* 20 *tl, bl,*
21 *t,* 24–25 *b,* 28 *tl,* 29, 44 *t, br,* 45 *bl,* 55, 64; **Chris Forsey** 4 *tl,* 5 *br,* 59 *cr;* **Nicholas Forder** 7, 13 *tr;*
Haywood Art Group 60 *cl;* **Christian Hook** 3 *tr,* 9 *tr,* 39 *tl;* **Michael Johnson** 1, 12–13 *b,* 34–35 *b,* 43,
50–51; **Maltings Partnership** 6 *br,* 11 *tl,* 47 *c,* 60 *bc,* 61 *br;* **Simon Mendez** 3 *b,* 8, 10–11 *b,* 14 *bl,* 16,
18 *bl,* 22 *b,* 32–33 *b,* 33 *t,* 38 *br,* 39 *b,* 48 *bl,* 49 *b,* 53 *bc,* 58–59, 62 *br, bl,* 63 *b;* **Eric Robson** 40 *tl;*
Jon Rogers 41; **M Taylor** 49 *tl;* 63 *cr*

The publishers would also like to thank the following
for supplying photographs for this book:

b = bottom, c = center, l = left, r = right, t = top

Pages: **4** *bl* Planet Earth Pictures; **6** *cl* Rex Features/Sipa Press; **9** *c* Corbis UK/Sean Sexton Collection, *cr*
Robert Harding Picture Library/Adam Woolfitt; **11** *tr* Rex Features/Iwasa; **13** *tl* Corbis UK/Reuter; **14** *tl*
Rex Features/Hojciech Dadej; **17** *br* Rex Features/Houston Post/Sipa/Michael Boddy; **18** *tl* Rex
Features/Sipa; **21** *br* ET Archive/Bibliothèque Nationale; **23** *br* Rex Features/Blondin; **25** *cr*
Popperfoto/Reuters; **26** *br* Corbis UK; **28** *br* Still Pictures/Hartmut Schwarzbach; **31** *bc* Rex Features; **32** *tr*
FirePix International; **35** *tl* Popperfoto/UPI; **37** *cr* Mary Evans Picture Library; **38** *tr* Still Pictures/Al Grillo;
40 *bl* Popperfoto/Jason Reed/Reuters, *br* Popperfoto/Mazlan Enjah/Reuter; **42** *br* Popperfoto; **45** *cr* Corbis
UK/Bettmann/UPI; **47** *tr* Robert Harding Picture Library; *br* Still Pictures/Mark Carwardine; **49** *tr* Tony
Stone Images/Cameron Davidson; **51** *tr* Still Pictures/Mark Edwards; **52** Science Photo Library/Dr Kari
Lounatmaa; **53** *cr* Popperfoto/Reuters/Corinne Dufka; **55** *tl* Still Pictures/John Maier; **56** *tl* Popperfoto; **57** *br*
Science Photo Library/David Parker; **58** *tr* Galaxy Picture Library/David Brown

Every effort has been made to trace the copyright holders of the photographs.
The publishers apologize for any inconvenience caused.